Shannon Miller
Olympic Gymnastics Legend

Shannon Miller
Olympic Gymnastics Legend

By Emily Pullman

GymnStars Volume 9

Creative Publishing

Creative Media, Inc.
PO Box 6270
Whittier, California 90609-6270
United States of America

The scanning, uploading, and distribution of this book via the Internet or via any other means without the permission of the publisher is illegal and punishable by law. Please purchase only authorized electronic editions and do not participate in or encourage electronic piracy of copyrighted materials. Your support of the authors' rights is appreciated.

The publisher does not have any control and does not assume any responsibility for author or third-party website or their content.

www.creativemedia.net

Book & cover design by Joseph Dzidrums

Copyright © 2016 by Creative Media, Inc. All rights reserved. Printed in the United States of America.

First Edition: August 2016

LCCN: On File

ISBN 978-1-938438-91-2
eISBN: 978-1-938438-92-9

Table of Contents

Chapter One
Sibling Revelry   7

Chapter Two
Gymnast   13

Chapter Three
Barcelona   19

Chapter Four
Golden Dreams   25

Chapter Five
Legend   31

Essential Links
                                                  37

About the Publisher
                                                  38

"I just loved being in the gym. I went one hour each week. When 60 minutes was up, they couldn't pry me from the gym."

Chapter One
Sibling Revelry

There are no secrets to success. It requires endless preparation, hard work, and the admirable ability to bounce back from failure. Because gymnast Shannon Miller possessed all these qualities, she became one of the most successful athletes of all time.

Shannon Lee Miller was born on March 10, 1977, in Rolla, Missouri. She eventually became the middle child in her family with an older sister named Tessa and a younger brother, Troy. Shannon's parents, Claudia and Ron Miller, met while attending Trinity University in San Antonio, Texas.

When Shannon was just a few months old, her family moved to Edmond, Oklahoma, where her father accepted a job as a professor of physics at the University of Central Oklahoma. Meanwhile, Shannon's mother worked as a bank vice president.

Located slightly north of Oklahoma City, Edmond is the Sooner State's sixth largest city. The Millers adored the "Crown Jewel of Oklahoma," and they settled comfortably in their new home.

Around the same time, Shannon's pediatrician noticed a problem with the development of the young girl's legs. They turned inward rather than growing straight. To correct the problem, an orthopedic surgeon recommended that Shannon wear leg braces for a year. Her parents and doctors initially feared the setback might delay their daughter's crawling and walking milestones, but thankfully, she developed at a normal pace.

BY Emily **Pullman**

Like many young children, Shannon worshipped her oldest sibling. The child wanted to be just like Tessa and emulated her sister in every way imaginable.

When Tessa was six years old, she began attending a nearby ballet class. Of course, Shannon demanded lessons, too. Once a week, she would pull on white tights, a colorful leotard, a springy tutu, and ballet slippers. Then, the excited youngster would head to a nearby studio with her sister.

After several sessions, though, the girls quickly grew bored with ballet. The highly energetic children desire a more fast-paced activity. In actuality, the Miller sisters craved a sports-related hobby. They eventually quit their dance lessons and began searching for a brand new interest to pursue.

When Shannon was five years old, she desperately wanted a trampoline for Christmas. The young girl thrilled at the thought of flying high in the sky and performing daring flips in the air. It would almost feel like flying.

The Miller sisters were thrilled when their parents reluctantly bought them a trampoline. They quickly mastered the springy apparatus. In fact, Claudia and Ron felt so frightened by some of their daughters' thrilling flips that they enrolled them in gymnastics lessons so they would not get hurt.

"It was a way to keep us from killing ourselves at home on my parent's furniture," Shannon joked to the *Elite Access* web series.

Shannon loved gymnastics right off the bat. In fact, she loved every part of the demanding sport, but the tiny youngster enjoyed tumbling more than anything. Her expressive eyes would shine with exhilaration when she watched more experienced gymnasts perform exciting moves on different apparatuses, like vault, balance beam, uneven bars, and especially the daunting floor exercise.

Whenever Shannon walked into the busy gym for a new lesson, a burst of excitement tingled inside her. The smitten athlete loved training inside the bustling gym filled with tumbling

by Emily **Pullman**

athletes and soaring gymnastics. The place felt like home to her.

One thing was clear. Shannon Miller had been bitten by the gymnastics bug. She was a gymnast now. The love of the sport would stick with her for the rest of her life.

"I excelled in learning skills, and I just had this voracious appetite for learning."

Chapter Two
Gymnast

Shannon and Tessa took gymnastics classes once a week. After several weeks of successful lessons, their instructor, Jerry Clavier, noticed the girls had enormous potential. As a result, he asked the sisters to begin attending classes one hour a day, five days a week.

"Please, please, please," little Shannon begged her parents. "Let me take more gymnastics lessons."

Meanwhile, Tessa remained silent during Shannon's exchange with their mother and father. The idea of increasing the amount of lessons didn't exactly appeal to her. In fact, the possibility helped the young girl reevaluate her dedication to the sport. She liked gymnastics, but did she love it?

The older sister quickly realized that she was not interested in making the extra commitment to the sport. Instead, Tessa asked for swimming and art lessons.

However, Shannon rose to the challenge of the increased time in the gym. For the first time in her life, the young girl had not followed her sister's lead. She had made her own choice - gymnastics - and loved it.

Shannon was a diligent worker at the gym. She thrived in the sport and progressed rapidly through various gymnastics classes. Despite her young age and small size, she acquired skills that older gymnasts had been trying to attain for years.

"I was in love," Shannon recalled on *Elite Access*. "You get to jump in a pit. You jump on a trampoline, swing on the monkey bars. What's not to love?"

When Shannon was seven years old, she passed the United States Association of Independent Gymnastics Clubs (USAIGC) rigorous testing program. As a reward for her accomplishment, she was invited to attend Bela Karolyi's gymnastics camp in Houston, Texas.

BY Emily Pullman

Bela was the most famous coach in the world. He had guided the legendary Nadia Comaneci to a perfect score at the Olympic Games, a sporting competition featuring the world's best athletes competing for top honors. He also led Mary Lou Retton to an all-around gold medal at the 1984 Olympics. While at the camp, Shannon simply listened to Bela and the other coaches and performed to the best of her ability. The hardworking approach would serve her well throughout her entire career.

At age nine, Shannon traveled with a North American delegation to the Soviet Union for a gymnastics camp. She quickly realized that the country had exceedingly high expectations for their gymnasts. At first, the young American struggled to complete the difficult skills that the Soviet coaches expected of her. However, she never lost her strong resolve and became determined to reach their accelerated level.

When Shannon returned to Oklahoma, she made an important change in her training. She began working with coach Steve Nunno, who had also traveled to the Soviet Union as part of the delegation. Steve owned Dynamo Gymnastics in Norman, Oklahoma. He was a tough coach who expected 100% from his gymnasts every day.

In 1989, Shannon competed at her biggest competition to date, the U.S. Olympic Festival. Hosted by the United States Olympic Committee, the amateur sporting event in Colorado Springs, Colorado, simulated the Olympic experience for young athletes with everything from Opening Ceremonies to medal presentations. The dynamo from Oklahoma placed third in the prestigious event.

Cincinnati, Ohio, hosted the 1991 U.S. Gymnastics Championships. The competition featured the best gymnasts in the country competing for top honors. Shannon placed seventh in the all-around event. More impressively, she captured gold on the balance beam and finished third on the vault.

Three months later, Shannon competed in her first world meet. At the 1991 World Championships in Indianapolis, Indiana, the rising gymnast won two silver medals. She helped

BY Emily **Pullman**

Team USA secure a second-place finish in the team event and won an individual silver medal on the balance beam competition.

Surrounded by many powerful, muscular gymnasts, Shannon's petite frame and balletic look made her a stand-out on the American team. Judges loved her lithe look and strong technical skills. Shannon's performances were further enhanced by her graceful, elegant style.

Sadly, dreams of competing at a consecutive worlds were dashed at the 1992 American Cup when Shannon suffered an uncharacteristic fall during her floor exercise. Due to injury, the gymnast missed the Individual Apparatus World Championships in Paris.

Refusing to let the missed opportunity discourage her, Shannon rebounded in a huge way. The determined gymnast shocked many when she won the 1992 Olympic Trials title over her top rival, Kim Zmeskal.

The girl from Edmond, Oklahoma, was heading to the Olympic Games in Barcelona. The world had better be ready for her!

*"I was very shy.
I didn't have great self-esteem
outside the gym. Gymnastics was
where I could shine."*

Chapter Three
Barcelona

Shannon Miller arrived in Barcelona as a strong medal threat in the gymnastics event. She left the country as the most decorated American athlete at the games. In all, she won five Olympic medals.

The Oklahoman performed brilliantly in the team event rarely setting a foot wrong. Her efforts helped the Americans secure a team bronze medal behind the winning Unified Team and Romania, the second place finishers. Besides Shannon, the American team also consisted of Wendy Bruce, Dominique Dawes, Betty Okino, Keri Strug, and world champion Kim Zmeskal.

In the all-around competition, Shannon missed out on the gold medal by the closest margin in Olympic history. She finished 0.012 points behind the Unified Team's Tatiana Gutsu. Her coach, Steve Nunno, felt Shannon was robbed of the gold medal by unfair judging, but the gymnast didn't let the controversy rattle her.

"For me, it wasn't losing a gold medal," she later remarked. "It was winning silver."

Shannon continued her strong showing in the event finals. The fifteen-year-old captured three more individual medals: a silver on balance beam and bronze medals on floor and uneven bars. Her Olympic medal count was higher than any other American's total in any sport at the games.

When Shannon returned to the United States, she was treated as an American hero. The teenager received multiple national and local honors. President George H.W. Bush honored her achievements at the White House, and the U.S. Senate presented her with a resolution honoring her Olympic achievement. Meanwhile, Edmond threw a grand parade in her honor.

The following year, Shannon traveled to Birmingham, England, for the 1993 World Gymnastics Championships. The competition marked the first time that the American entered a world event as the overwhelming favorite. Undaunted by the pressure, the teenager seized

BY Emily **Pullman**

three gold medals: all-around, uneven bars, and the floor exercise final.

Shannon's spectacular performances inspired American television commentator Kathy Johnson to remark that the American was the most dominant gymnast since the renowned Nadia Comăneci. High praise, indeed. In actuality, Shannon may have earned an additional medal at the competition had she not withdrawn from the vault event due to an illness.

One year later, at the 1994 World Championships in Brisbane, Australia, Shannon won a second consecutive all-around title. The consistent American defeated the silver medalist, Romania's Lavinia Miloşovici, and Russia's Dina Kotchetkova, who placed a distant third. She also took first place on the balance beam with a nearly flawless exercise.

Shannon went undefeated for over a year before her streak was snapped. At the 1994 Goodwill Games, Kotchetkova narrowly defeated Miller by .057 points. Despite the disappointing loss, Shannon recovered by netting gold medals on the balance beam and floor exercise. She also scored vault and uneven bars silver medals.

Two weeks later, Shannon flew to Nashville, Tennessee, to compete at the 1994 U.S. Championships. Although she performed well, she didn't win. The gymnast scored five silver medals behind Dominique Dawes in every event.

Shannon Miller had competed, toured, and made media appearances non-stop for over two years. It was a grueling schedule for anyone, especially for a teenager trying to balance a school schedule with a sports career. Had she retired then, she would still be remembered as one of America's greatest gymnasts ever.

Yet, the 1996 Atlanta Olympics were just two years away. Shannon's impressive resume lacked only one major title: an Olympic gold medal. Did she want to keep training for the next games?

Her answer was a resounding yes. Shannon vowed to compete in Atlanta, and when she put her mind to something, it happened.

by Emily Pullman

Silver In Barcelona

"I'm competing for perfection every single time."

Chapter Four
Golden Dreams

By the time the 1996 Olympics arrived, Shannon Miller had become the most decorated American gymnast in history. She had also graduated from Edmond North High School and begun attending college at the University of Oklahoma.

Shannon also had experienced a difficult two-year run up to the Olympics. An ankle injury hampered her performance during the 1995 season culminating in a loss at nationals to thirteen-year-old Dominique Moceanu. The 1995 World Championships presented quite a challenge as well when for the first time ever, she walked away from worlds without a single individual medal.

1996 began as quite a challenge too. Shannon struggled with two major injuries. She suffered from tendinitis in her left wrist, an ongoing problem that affected her training on the uneven bars to a large extent. The teenager also had a pulled hamstring that limited her overall training regime.

Not wanting to irritate her serious injuries further, Shannon chose to not attend the 1996 World Championships in San Juan, Puerto, that spring. Suffering an injury of her own, Shannon's biggest American rival, Dominique Moceanu, also skipped the event due to a stress fracture.

Despite the physical setbacks, Shannon prevailed at the 1996 U.S. National Championships in Knoxville, Tennessee. Relying on muscle memory, years of experience, and sheer grit, the talented gymnast overcame some early struggles in the event to rally back with strong routines on day two of the competition. Her efforts earned her America's all-around crown for the second time in her career. When she learned of her victory, the modest athlete flashed an appreciative grin.

"I had a rough beam routine, so I had to come back," she admitted to NBC. "But mainly I was trying to focus on doing all my new skills and they came out well, so that's good."

BY Emily **Pullman**

Still cautious about her pair of injuries, Shannon opted to withdraw from the 1996 Olympic Trials. USA Gymnastics would simply substitute her nationals' tally for her score at trials. If Shannon's total finished in the top six at trials, the star gymnast would head to Atlanta. In the end, her score held up strongly. On June 30, 1996, Shannon Miller was officially named to her second-straight Olympic team.

By mid-summer, Shannon felt ready to compete in her second Olympics. On July 21, she and her teammates lit up the Georgia Dome with strong performances in the optionals round. Their terrific efforts placed them second overall with one final day of competition remaining.

On July 23, Shannon led the United States' gymnastics squad to the first-ever team title in American history. The well-rounded gymnasts unleashed thrilling, memorable routines that garnered rock-star applause from the thrilled crowd on hand to watch the historic achievement. Their win was given a dramatic tinge when Keri Strug stuck her landing on a vault while injured in the final performance of the competition.

Shannon Miller: *Olympic Gymnastics Legend*

    The world promptly fell in love with the American women's gymnastics team. The seven gymnasts, dubbed The Magnificent Seven, became overnight celebrities. The squad, Shannon Miller, Dominique Moceanu, Dominique Dawes, Kerri Strug, Amy Chow, Amanda Borden, and Jaycie Phelps, had also become quite close during the Atlanta Games. For the rest of the life they would be bound by their momentous accomplishment.

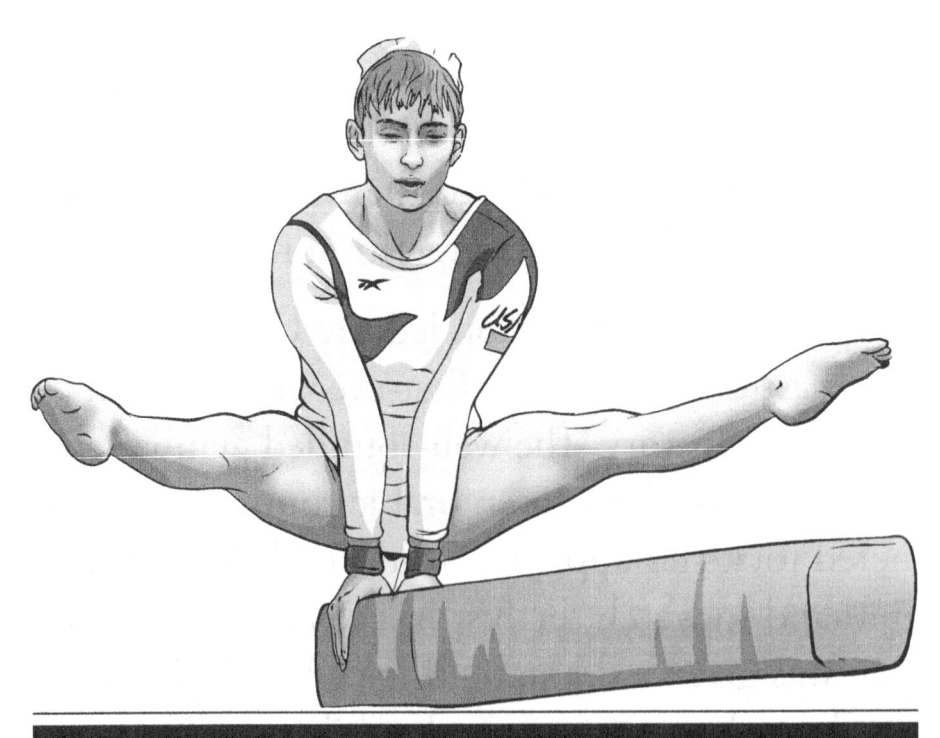

Balance Beam Queen

BY Emily **Pullman**

On July 29, the top eight gymnasts advanced to the balance beam final. After a disappointing all-around performance, it was Shannon's last chance to win an individual gold medal.

Not surprisingly, the courageous athlete gave a spectacular performance on the apparatus. Then, she waited through several competitors' routines to see if she had won. Despite strong efforts by all-around champion Lilia Podkopayeva and Romania's Gina Gogean, Shannon ultimately won the balance beam competition. The new Olympic champion smiled brightly upon learning she had earned her long-awaited individual gold medal.

The American crowd was so excited by Shannon's victory that their enthusiastic cheers lasted several minutes. When they roared for the gymnast to take a curtain call, she acknowledged the crowd with a heartfelt wave.

"No one deserves this more than you," Coach Steve Nunno told the smiling gymnast.

It was difficult for anyone to argue with that statement.

"Goal setting is a huge part of my life."

Chapter Five
Legend

Shannon concluded her gymnastics career with seven Olympic medals. To this day, she remains the most accomplished American gymnast ever. Her impressive tally also includes eight world championships medals and countless national and international medals.

Even more impressively, Miller ruled gymnastics while maintaining an "A" average in school while balancing various other responsibilities. Her parents always stressed the importance of a good education.

In 2003, Shannon earned a B.B.A. in Marketing and Entrepreneurship from the University of Houston. Four years later, she graduated from Boston College Law School.

In 2006, Shannon relocated from Oklahoma to Jacksonville, Florida. She often makes appearances at gymnastics centers where the much-admired figure delivers motivational speeches to young athletes. In addition, the Olympic champion conducts balance beam clinics for budding gymnasts.

On August 25, 2008, Shannon married businessman John Falconetti. The couple had met at a celebrity golf tournament and instantly hit it off. After a beautiful ceremony, the happy pair honeymooned in Italy.

Several months later, Shannon and John received the blissful news that they would become parents. On October 28, 2009, the couple welcomed a son into their lives. John Rocco Falconetti, born at 6:46 p.m., weighed a healthy 7 pounds, 11 ounces.

In December of 2010, Shannon received devastating news about her health. Doctors diagnosed her with a germ-cell malignant tumor, a type of ovarian cancer. Her gynecologist discovered the growth in a pelvic exam during a routine physical, proving that maintaining regular doctor checkups can save lives.

During surgery, doctors removed a baseball-sized cyst from one of Shannon's ovaries. Fortunately, because the cancer was caught early, surgeons removed all of the cancer. Afterward, the athlete underwent nine weeks of chemotherapy, an aggressive treatment that uses medicine to destroy cancer cells.

Shannon approached her cancer management like she once prepared for a major competition. She broke down her treatments by concentrating on them one week at a time. Using this method, along with eating well, exercising, and blogging on her website, helped make the chemotherapy more bearable.

"After my cancer diagnosis, I slowly began listening to those words that had guided me through so many pivotal moments in my life," she told *Cancer Forward*. "They became my rallying cry, my mantra. You fall down, you get back up."

In September of 2011, doctors gave Shannon a clean bill of health. Determined to spread the word about the importance of early cancer detection, the grateful survivor became an advocate for women's health. She often spoke to women about the importance of scheduling regular doctor visits and paying attention to one's body so even the earliest symptoms can be detected. The Olympic champion was happy to share her knowledge with anyone who might benefit from the information.

On January 14, 2013, Miller announced that she and husband were expecting their second child. Their daughter, Sterling Diane Falconetti, was born on June 25, 2013.

"I have been blessed to have the opportunity to do some amazing things in my life, but being a mom is second to none," the beloved Olympian announced in a statement released on her official website *ShannonMiller.com*.

These days, Shannon's professional focus rests squarely on her website and radio show entitled *Shannon Miller Lifestyle: Health & Fitness for Women*. The project uses her voice, trials, and triumphs to assist women in making their health a priority. Designed for women of all ages and backgrounds, the website encourages a supportive environment for women where they can ask questions about their health. The gymnast has also produced lifestyle books, cook books, and fitness DVDs under the name.

by Emily **Pullman**

Golden Girl

"As a woman, health and wellness spoke to me," Shannon revealed to the *Trending Now* web series. "We're dedicated to helping women make their health a priority."

Of course, gymnastics remains Shannon's number one professional love. She continues to be in high demand in gymnastics by serving as a commentator for sporting events and a spokesperson for the sport and its related products. The athlete has also worked as an Olympic analyst for *MSNBC, NBC HD,* and *Yahoo! Sports.*

Today, Shannon's legacy is highly respected by gymnastics professionals and fans. She is a proud member of the USA Gymnastics Hall of Fame, the U.S. Olympic Committee Hall of Fame, the International Gymnastics Hall of Fame, and the Women's International Sports Hall of Fame.

The little girl from Edmond, Oklahoma, has come a long way since she followed her sister to ballet and gymnastics classes. World champion. Olympic champion. Cancer survivor. Motivational Speaker. Lifestyle guru. Shannon Miller has proved time and again that she has the golden touch.

Essential Links

Shannon Miller Lifestyle Health & Fitness for Women
www.ShannonMiller.com/lifestyle-home

Official Facebook
facebook.com/ShannonMillerOfficial

Official Twitter Account
twitter.com/shannonmiller96

Official Pinterest
pinterest.com/ShannonMiller96

Official Instagram
instagram.com/shannonmiller96

Official YouTube Channel
youtube.com/user/SMlifestyle

Shannon Miller Leotard Collection
aerialsbyalphafactor.com/shannon-miller

USA Gymnastics
usagym.org

About the Publisher

Creative Media Publishing has produced biographies on several inspiring personalities: *Simone Biles, Nadia Comaneci, Clayton Kershaw, Mike Trout, Yuna Kim, Shawn Johnson, Nastia Liukin, The Fierce Five, Gabby Douglas, Sutton Foster, Kelly Clarkson, Idina Menzel, Missy Franklin* and more. They've published two award-winning Young Adult novels, *Cutters Don't Cry* (Moonbeam Children's Book Award) and *Kaylee: The "What If?" Game* (Children's Literary Classic Awards). They have also produced a line of popular children's book series, including *The Creeper and the Cat, Future Presidents Club, Princess Dessabelle* and *Quinn: The Ballerina*.

www.CreativeMedia.net
@CMIPublishing

Build Your GymnStars™ Collection Today!

Now sports fans can learn about gymnastics' greatest stars! Americans **Shawn Johnson** and **Nastia Liukin** became the darlings of the 2008 Beijing Olympics when the fearless gymnasts collected 9 medals between them. Four years later at the 2012 London Olympics, America's **Fab Five** claimed gold in the team competition. A few days later, **Gabby Douglas** added another gold medal to her collection when she became the fourth American woman in history to win the Olympic all-around title. The *GymnStars* series reveals these gymnasts' long, arduous path to Olympic glory. *Gabby Douglas: Golden Smile, Golden Triumph* received a **2012 Moonbeam Children's Book Award**.

Build Your SkateStars™ Collection Today!

At the 2010 Vancouver Olympics, tragic circumstances thrust **Joannie Rochette** into the spotlight when her mother died two days before the ladies short program. Joannie then captured hearts everywhere by courageously skating two moving programs to win the Olympic bronze medal. *Joannie Rochette: Canadian Ice Princess* profiles the popular figure skater's moving journey.

Meet figure skating's biggest star: **Yuna Kim**. The Korean trailblazer produced two legendary performances at the 2010 Vancouver Olympic Games to win the gold medal. *Yuna Kim: Ice Queen* uncovers the compelling story of how the beloved figure skater overcame poor training conditions, various injuries and numerous other obstacles to become world and Olympic champion.

Y Not Girl™
Women Who Inspire!

Our **YNot Girl** series chronicles the lives and careers of the world's most famous role models. **Jennie Finch: Softball Superstar** details the California native's journey from a shy youngster to softball's most famous face. In **Kelly Clarkson: Behind Her Hazel Eyes**, young readers will find inspiration reading about the superstar's rise from a broke waitress with big dreams to becoming one of the recording industry's top musical acts. **Missy Franklin: Swimming Sensation** narrates the Colorado native's transformation from a talented swimming toddler to queen of the pool.

StageStars™
Broadway's Best!

Theater fans first fell for **Sutton Foster** in her triumphant turn as *Thoroughly Modern Millie*. Since then the triple threat has charmed Broadway audiences by playing a writer, a princess, a movie star, a nightclub singer, and a Transylvania farm girl. Now the two-time Tony winner is conquering television in the acclaimed series *Bunheads*. A children's biography, ***Sutton Foster: Broadway Sweetheart, TV Bunhead*** details the role model's rise from a tiny ballerina to the toast of Broadway and Hollywood.

Idina Menzel's career has been "Defying Gravity" for years! With starring roles in *Wicked* and *Rent*, the Tony-winner is one of theater's most beloved performers. The powerful vocalist has also branched out in other mediums. She has filmed a recurring role on television's smash hit *Glee* and lent her talents to the Disney films, *Enchanted* and *Frozen*. A children's biography, ***Idina Menzel: Broadway Superstar*** narrates the actress' rise to fame from a Long Island wedding singer to overnight success!

Fair Youth
Emylee of Forest Springs

Twelve-year-old Emylee Markette has felt invisible her entire life. Then one fateful afternoon, three beautiful sisters arrive in her sleepy New England town and instantly become the most popular girls at Forest Springs Middle School. To everyone's surprise, the Fay sisters befriend Emylee and welcome her into their close-knit circle. Before long, the shy loner finds herself running with the cool crowd, joining the track team and even becoming friends with her lifelong crush.

Through it all, though, Emylee's weighed down by nagging suspicions. Why were the Fay sisters so anxious to befriend her? How do they know some of her inner thoughts? What do they truly want from her?

When Emylee eventually discovers that her new friends are secretly fairies, she finds her life turned upside down yet again and must make some life-changing decisions.

Fair Youth: Emylee of Forest Springs marks the first volume in an exciting new book series.

Future Presidents Club
Girls Rule!

Ashley Moore wants to know why there's never been a girl president. Before long the inspired six-year-old creates a special, girls-only club - the **Future Presidents Club**. Meet five enthusiastic young girls who are ready to change the world. *Future Presidents Club: Girls Rule* is the first book in a series about girls making a difference!

Princess Dessabelle
Makes a Friend

Meet **Princess Dessabelle**, a spoiled, lonely princess with a quick temper.

In *Princess Dessabelle Makes a Friend*, the lonely youngster discovers the meaning of true friendship. *Princess Dessabelle: Tennis Star* finds the pampered girl learning the importance of good sportsmanship.

Quinn the Ballerina
The Sleeping Beauty!

Quinn
The Ballerina
The Sleeping Beauty

BY CHRISTINE **DZIDRUMS**

Quinn the Ballerina can hardly believe it's finally performance day. She's playing her first principal role in a production of *The Sleeping Beauty*.

Yet, Quinn is also nervous. Can she really dance the challenging steps? Will people believe her as a cursed princess caught in a 100-year spell?

Join Quinn as she transforms into Princess Aurora in an exciting retelling of Tchaikovsky's *The Sleeping Beauty*. Now you can relive, or experience for the first time, one of ballet's most acclaimed works as interpreted by a 9 year old.

Magical Reboots
Rapunzel

From the popular new series, ***Classical Reboots, Rapunzel*** updates the **Brothers Grimm** fairy tale with hilarious and heartbreaking results.

Rapunzel has been locked in her adoptive mother's attic for years. Just as the despondent teenager abandons hope of escaping her private prison, a mysterious tablet computer appears. Before long, Rapunzel's quirky fairy godmother, Aiko, has the conflicted young girl questioning her place in the world.

The SoCal Series

Cutters Don't Cry

2010 Moonbeam Children's Book Award Winner! In a series of raw journal entries written to her absentee father, a teenager chronicles her penchant for self-harm, a serious struggle with depression and an inability to vocally express her feelings.

Kaylee: The 'What If?' Game

"I play the 'What If?'" game all the time. It's a cruel, wicked game."

When free spirit Kaylee suffers a devastating loss, her personality turns dark as she struggles with depression and unresolved anger. Can Kaylee repair her broken spirit, or will she remain a changed person?

Made in the USA
Monee, IL
24 March 2025